Library of
Davidson College

Series / Number 90-004

Weak Parliaments and Military Coups in Africa: *A Study in Regime Instability*

JAY E. HAKES

Louisiana State University in New Orleans

SAGE PUBLICATIONS / Beverly Hills / London

Copyright © 1973 by Sage Publications, Inc.

Printed in the United States of America

All rights reserved. No part of this book may be reproduced or utilized in any form or by any means, electronic or mechanical, including photocopying, recording, or by any information storage and retrieval system, without permission in writing from the publisher.

328.3
H155w

For information address:

SAGE PUBLICATIONS, INC.
275 South Beverly Drive
Beverly Hills, California 90212

SAGE PUBLICATIONS, INC.
St George's House / 44 Hatton Garden
London EC1N 8ER

International Standard Book Number 0-8039-0372-3

Library of Congress Catalog No. L.C. 73-89064

FIRST PRINTING

When citing a professional paper, please use the proper form. Remember to cite the correct Sage Professional Paper series title and include the paper number. One of the two following formats can be adapted (depending on the style manual used):

(1) KORNBERG, A. et al. (1973) "Legislatures and Societal Change: The Case of Canada." Sage Research Papers in the Social Sciences (Comparative Legislative Studies Series, No. 90-002). Beverly Hills and London: Sage Pubns.

OR

(2) Kornberg, Allan et al. 1973. *Legislatures and Societal Change: The Case of Canada.* Sage Research Papers in the Social Sciences, vol. 1, series no. 90-002 (Comparative Legislative Studies Series). Beverly Hills and London: Sage Publications.

75-10187

Contents

Methodology *10*

Salience and Legislative Activity *13*

Accountability and Elections *25*

Conclusions *32*

WEAK PARLIAMENTS AND MILITARY COUPS IN AFRICA:
A Study in Regime Instability

JAY E. HAKES

Louisiana State University in New Orleans

Perhaps the most fundamental function of legislative institutions is that of legitimating governmental authority. By representing a population, or at least the politically relevant parts of a population, a legislature can generate popular support both for the specific policies that it adopts or ratifies and for the political system of which it is a part. In fact, one of the prime stimuli to the growth of legislative institutions in the West has been the need of governments to obtain popular approval for policies such as the collection of taxes. Legislatures are an important part of the legitimating process that endows governmental decisions with moral oughtness. Their Latin origins suggest the initimate relationship between words such as legislature, legitimacy, and legality.

Although legislatures are to some extent of Western derivation, both historically and etymologically, a relationship between legislatures and legitamacy has been recognized in the Third World, where legislative bodies are often new and weak structures and the level of citizen participation and awareness are often low, compared to North America and Europe.[1] Ralph Crow (1970: 300-301) considers this issue when discussing the political role of the Lebanese Chamber of Deputies. He states:

> (The president) must give constant attention to the Chamber, the members of which are there because they have demonstrated their (political) strength. The president needs to satisfy at least their minimal demands or he will be faced with a stalemate. In this fashion support is marshalled for the government of the day, and legitimacy, however tenuous, is maintained...

AUTHOR'S NOTE: The author wishes to acknowledge the helpful advice of John K. Wildgen in the preparation of this paper.

The Chamber of Deputies is the main "transmission box" where the executive's need for political support and the society's demands are brought together, meshed and harmonized.

In addition, Robert Packenham (1970: 527-528) devotes considerable attention to the legitimating function of the Brazilian National Congress. In this connection he says:

The Brazilian Congress. . .performed a latent legitimizing function insofar as its activities had the consequence of legitimizing the government in power at the time, even beyond what was intended or understood by the legislators. Simply by meeting regularly and uninterruptedly, the legislature produced, among the relevant populace and elites, a wider and deeper sense of the government's moral right to rule than would otherwise have obtained.

Finally, Newell Stultz (1970: 332) makes similar conclusions in his study of the Kenya National Assembly:

Parliament in Kenya has to some extent performed 'political' functions, notably in the reduction of cleavage, the ventilation of grievances and, more especially, the legitimization of the political system.

Even where legislative institutions play only a weak role in decision-making, some connection between them and the generation of public support can usually be found. Otherwise, strong executives would have little reason for going through the inconvenience of having their policies ratified by representative assemblies.

In general theories of political systems, two properties of legislatures are regarded as promoting support for political authorities. First, legislatures usually operate because they are constitutionally required. Thus, the regular operation of the legislature is a symbol of constitutionalism. Constitutionalism, in turn, promotes the legitimacy of authorities, because "any measure taken to invest the authorities with greater validity because of their conformity with the regime will serve to increase the input of diffuse support on their behalf" (Easton, 1965: 301). Although constitutionalism is in many countries not firmly established, even where support for it is weak, it is an important variable affecting political behavior. Second, legislatures can generate support, because they are by formal prescription representative structures. Easton (1965: 252-256) attributes a stress-reducing function to representation, both formal and informal. For theoretical reasons at least, then, we should expect that some of the burden of legitimating a civilian regime will fall on its legislature.

In Africa, as in many parts of the world, governmental authority does not in this century seem to have been legitimated very well, at least if we assume that regime instability is an indication of difficulties in obtaining popular support and loyalty from a citizenry. Through the 1950's and early 1960's Africa was ruled by outside colonial powers, who, in the main, "owed their presence and their claim to legitimacy to force.... The chain of authority from the top downwards was untouched by any principle of representation or consultation (First, 1972: 29, 31).

In the years since independence, about half of the new civilian regimes of sub-Saharan Africa have been toppled by military intervention. The ease with which these extraconstitutional changes of power were accomplished seemed to indicate that the outgoing regimes had generated less popular support than was previously assumed by observers of African politics. It is difficult to provide a satisfactory explanation of why so many regimes lost legitimacy and were overthrown. Aristide R. Zolberg (1968b: 70) says:

> With little regard for the comfort of social scientists, the incidence of conflict and disorder (in tropical Africa) appears unrelated to such variables as type of colonial experience, size, number of parties, absolute level or rate of economic and social development, as well as to the overall characteristics of regimes.

Nevertheless, if legislatures are supposed to legitimate governmental authority, it would seem that parliamentary institutions in Africa must share some of the responsiblity for the widespread failure of civilian regimes to generate popular support and to insure their own persistence.

To posit a relationship between the ability of legislatures to generate popular support and regime persistence in Africa assumes, in the first place, that the public is aware of the existence of the legislature, can distinguish it from other governmental structures, and is affected by its behavior. This proposition seems, initially, to be rather dubious, in part because in states where legislative bodies are new and the percentage of literates in the population is low, public awareness of legislative behavior is probably also low. Despite an absence of empirical data, however, it is likely that all nations have "attentive publics," as have been identified in studies of Western democracies (Boynton et al., 1969 and Patterson et al., 1973). However small, attentive publics are aware of and affected by the activity of legislatures and usually have a disproportionate impact on politics. Even if the "popular support" generated for regimes by legislatures is confined to highly educated, narrowly based elites, this support is significant politically. The "attentive publics," in some cases, might even include foreign governments, who follow closely political events in new states, often their former colonies, and possess the capability of affecting the success of coup attempts.[2] Although this paper does not attempt to define exactly what part of the general populace is affected by parliamentary behavior, it does operate on the assumption that those elements that most influence regime stability are most likely to also be those who are aware of legislative activity.

A second assumption involved in the connection between the legislature's ability to generate popular support and regime persistence is that a relationship exists between popular attitudes toward the regime and the willingness of the military to intervene. Again, the proposition seems somewhat dubious, because virtually all coups have been motivated by the institutional interests and demands of the military itself. Soldiers, however, are not totally isolated from contact with civilian society, particularly in African nations, where the ties of extended family are still strong. Thus, the military is likely to share, to some extent, the attitudes of the socity of which it is a part. More importantly, the military's desire to stage a coup on behalf of its own interests is tempered by its perception of popular affection for the existing regime. Gutteridge (1972: 11) comments directly on the connection between military intervention and public support for the regime:

> While the desire of uniformed men to promote their interests has been expressed in the form of mutinies and outright seizures of political power, their success in the latter has been facilitated to a large extent by the decline in popularity of the civilian governments that came to power after independence. With the exception of Ghana in 1972, there is probably no instance in black Africa where the army attempted to seize power from a popularly elected

government, nor in places where the conduct of political actors was still regulated by the legitimate rules of political competition.

Thus, it seems to have been the combination of the self-interests of the armed forces and popular disaffection from the regime that has produced military coups.[3]

Analysis of the years preceding military coups in Africa, then, should contribute to our understanding of the roles of legislatures generally and on the African political scene. How do legislatures preform during times of great stress on the political system? What factors influence the ability of a legislature to generate popular support? Are legislatures so unimportant that their activities are epiphenomenal and without direct connection to the problem of regime persistance? Do active legislatures serve as barriers to attempts to undermine regimes? Can legislatures provide regimes with a reservoir of support that enables them to survive unpopular decisions and periods of crisis? Are coups inevitable if legislatures fail or cease to perform a legitimating function? These questions— all of which are important ones for the comparative analysis of legislative systems—can be studied with greater effectiveness in periods and systems characterized by disorders, crises and coups than in periods and systems with greater stability. Events in Africa over the last fifteen years or so, then, should be of considerable interest to students of comparative legislative systems.

Nonetheless, little is known about the performance of African legislatures during the periods that precede coups. Most of the literature on African parliaments deals with the first years of their operation and not with the hectic events leading to coups.[4] The reasons for this lacuna are not difficult to discern. In many cases civilian regimes increased restrictions on political research during their last years, and the coming to power of the military further inhibited research. Not surprisingly, many political scientists migrated to seek more hospitable research climates. A cynic might also suggest that academic constraints were as important as political ones. Political scientists in Africa were expected to study "political development." (The study of "political decay" had not even been named, let alone legitimated.) The break-up of civilian regimes hardly constituted development, so there was a tendency to exercise selective perception and ignore those aspects of political systems that did not fit preconceived models.[5] Whatever the reasons, there is a paucity of data on precoup politics that handicaps any attempt to assess carefully the role that legislative institutions play during such periods.

METHODOLOGY

The purpose of this paper is to propose directions in which analysis of parliamentary performance in the years preceding coups might proceed and to suggest some kinds of data that might furnish a basis for such analysis. The ideal study would include multivariate analysis of all states in Black Africa that enjoyed majority rule at some point in recent history. Multivariate analysis requires data that are extensive and reliable. Although recent important breakthroughs in the systematic collection of African data (Morrison et al., 1972) have encouraged increased use of multivariate analysis in African political studies, the quantity and quality of the data suggest that the testing of hypotheses should probably not be restricted to such an approach. The most serious difficulty is that the reliability of African data in general and team-collected data in particular is questionable enough to undermine confidence in results based on it.[6] As a result, the present study deals with a narrow range of variables and employs data with considerable caution.

Dependence on official parliamentary records for some kinds of information provides a second important constraint, since such records are available from only some of the African states.[7] Except for Sierra Leone, all of the Commonwealth states—Ghana, Nigeria, Tanzania, Uganda, Kenya, Malawi and Zambia. These seven cases comprise all Commonwealth states in sub-Saharan Africa receiving independence by 1965 for which parliamentary records have been continuously published.

As with most African states, stress on the political systems of our seven cases has resulted from factors such as ethnic cleavage and aspirations for rapid social and economic development. In all cases except Tanzania and Malawi, ethnic tension had led to major incidents of serious political stress and violence. According to one index (Taylor and Hudson, 1972: 271-273), five of our cases are among the twelve most ethnically fractionalized societies in the world. Table 1 gives a rough measure of ethnic fractionalization in the seven cases. The position of Tanzania as most fractionalized in the world is misleading, however, since national integration in this East Africa state is encouraged by the widespread use of Swahili as a lingua franca.

Social and economic development is a top priority in each state. Table 2 provides estimates of literacy, newspaper circulation and distribution of radios. Variables such as these not only help to measure development, but also help to define the outer parameters of who might constitute

Table 1. Ethnic Fractionalization in Anglophone Africa

	F Index
Tanzania	.93
Uganda	.90
Nigeria	.87
Kenya	.83
Zambia	.82
Ghana	.71
Malawi	.62

Source: Taylor and Hudson, 1972: 271-273

Table 2. Mass Communications Potential in Anglophone Africa

	Literacy 1965 (%)	Daily Newspaper Circulation per 1,000 Population, 1968	Radios per 1,000 Population, 1966
Zambia	40	70	14
Nigeria	33	90	12
Ghana	30	350	70
Uganda	30	80	61
Kenya	25	90	39
Tanzania	17	40	10
Malawi	10	0	29

Source: Morrison et al. (1972: 70, 78-79)

the public that is attentive to parliamentary behavior. For a study of regime instability, it is important to note that rapid expansion of literacy and communications can be a destabilizing force. (Lerner, 1958).

The dependent variable in the present study is regime instability. Military coups have been successful in three of our cases—Nigeria (1966), Ghana (1966), and Uganda (1971). In the other four states, civilian regimes have remained in power, although Kenya and Tanzania, along with Uganda, were struck in 1964 by military mutinies, which were put down with the help of British forces. Although a variety of factors undoubtedly contributed to the overthrow of regimes in Nigeria, Ghana and Uganda, we are particularly interested in the relationship, if any, between regime instability, regime legitimacy, and parlimentary performance.

It is reasonable to expect that the following situation would lead to coups in Nigeria, Ghana, and Uganda. Political regimes in these states should steadily lose popular support so that their legitimacy is at a low ebb at the time of a coup. In other words, these regimes should be less successful in generating support at the time of a coup than in earlier years. Moreover, they should also be less successful in this regard than regimes that have not experienced coups. If coups are preceded by a loss in regime legitimacy and legislatures are major agents in providing it, then certain patterns in parliamentary performance should recur. We should find that in Nigeria, Ghana, Uganda parliaments decline in their ability to provide legitimacy before the regimes are overthrown. In Tanzania, Kenya, Malawi, and Zambia parliaments should not have declined to the same extent. If such a pattern can be established, it would support, though not necessarily confirm, an argument that legislatures are important agents of legitimation and that the failure of legislatures to perform this function is conducive to regime instability. If no approximation of this pattern is found, then parliaments may be irrelevant to the study of regime instability.

The suggested relationship between African legislatures and regime instability is only speculative at this point, and it could be argued that legislatures do not have much impact on such matters. Moreover, it is difficult to resolve the question one way or the other, especially given the lack of survey data indicating public attitudes toward legislative institutions. Nonetheless, it is possible to define the relationship between parliaments and regime stability in such a way as to permit available data to be brought to bear. One approach might be to analyze the salience and the public accountability of legislatures as indicators of institutional capabilities for promoting legitimacy.

SALIENCE AND LEGISLATIVE ACTIVITY

Gerhard Loewenberg (1971: 190) who has explored several aspects of the relationship between parliament activity and regime stability in Europe states:

> On the assumption that the images which symbilize legitimacy derive at least in part from the structure of government, especially from the traditional structures conveying both legality and participation, we state as a...hypothesis that *the continuity and salience of parliament affect the durability of public support for the regime, which in turn affects regime stability.* [Italics added.]

Given the lack of survey data on public attitudes, both for the period under consideration by Loewenberg and for Africa, it is difficult to state with certainty much more than that the salience of legislative institutions is a necessary though not a sufficient condition for their performance of legitimating functions. That is, a legislature must be visible to the public in order to generate popular support, but such visibility is no guarantee that the legitimating function will be performed. Nonetheless, Loewenberg's hypothesis is a valuable one, for the association between the salience of parliaments and regime stability can be tested, thus permitting a somewhat indirect approach to the problem of regime legitimacy.

To be visible parliaments must meet. Some of the most modern and striking buildings in Anglophone Africa are those housing the chambers of its national parliaments. However, it is only when the chamber are occupied and parliamentary business is being conducted that the legislatures become visible in a meaningful snese. The style of press coverage of parliamentary proceedings in Anglophone Africa helps to produce a close relationship between meetings and visibility. Although newspapers in West Africa have been somewhat livelier in their reporting than those in East Africa, in general papers within Commonwealth Africa have adopted a British style of covering legislatures, that is, stories are confined to agenda for forthcoming meetings and summaries of debates and business conducted in previous meetings. In the daily press it is unlikely that meetings of parliament will not receive at least one substantial story, just as it is unlikely that articles about parliament as such will appear when parliament is out of session. Of course, the ability of the press to publicize the activity of parliaments varies greatly among our seven cases (see Table 2), and even under the most favorable of circumstances exposure would be limited to elites. Still, as discussed earlier, those who are able to follow parliamentary activity in the press should tend to overlap with those who have a significant impact on politics. In addition, in some states transmission of a "Day in Parliament" program on national radio can contribute to the publicizing of parliamentary meetings.

The suitability of using number of meetings as an operational definition of parliamentary visibility is enhanced by the tendency for number of meetings to correlate positively with other measures of parliamentary activity. It is possible that number of meetings might not reflect accurately the overall amount of parliamentary activity, since, in theory, the length of meetings could be variable. In practice, however, parliaments in Anglophone Africa have fixed schedules for their meetings so that time per meetings can, for all practical purposes, be treated as a constant within a given system. It would be surprising, then, if trends in parliamentary meetings were not closely related to other measures of parliamentary activity, such as number of bills passed and number of questions answered. In fact, the few data that are available suggest that the relationship is a strong one. Data on number of meetings, bills passed, and questions answered from four annual sessions of the Tanganyika parliament (Tordoff, 1967: 7) produces a Pearson's r of .77 for the relationship between meetings and bills and .98 for meetings and questions. Similar data on Ghana (Lee, 1963: 395) produces r's of .83 and .35 respectively.

The data for seven African countries indicate that there is not a simple correlation between annual number of meetings of parliaments and regime instability (see Table 3). Tanzania, for instance, has a parliament that has been inactive, relative to similar organs elsewhere in Anglophone Africa; the Bunge met on the average of only 39 days a year during the period 1961 to 1970. Yet Tanzania has experienced over ten years of independent, civilian rule, although it has not, of course, been marked by complete domestic tranquility. On the otherhand, Ghana and Uganda have, on the whole, had relatively active parliamentary institutions; they sat, on the average, 77 and 78 days per year respectively. However, this activity does not seem to have been an obstacle to the failure of their civilian regimes. These phenomena are not necessarily incompatible with the suggestion that parliamentary salience is associated with a regime's legitimacy. Other institutions, such as political parties, can also contribute to regime legitimacy. This is evidently the case in Tanzania,

Table 3. Annual Meetings of Parliaments in Anglophone Africa

Year	Ghana[a]	Nigeria[b]	Tanzania[c]	Uganda[d]	Kenya[e]	Malawi[f]	Zambia[g]
1957-58	85						
1958-59	87						
1959-60	94	44					
1960-61	97	54					
1961-62	75	41	34				
1962-63	61	39	29	92			
1963-64	66	32	26	83	90		
1964-65	48	38	24	83	95	19	58
1965-66	coup	coup	55	58	106	20	57
1966-67			49	87	119	16	33
1967-68			49	45	136	20	66
1968-69			42	68	89	14	62
1969-70			41	67	115	15	52
1970-71				coup		19	

a. *Daily Graphic* (1965-66); *Ghana Evening News* (1965-66); Ghana Natl. Assembly (1957-65); and Lee (1963: 394). For the first four years, the figures are based on sessions, which lasted approximately a year. After that point, they are based on 12-month periods from July 1, Republic Day. In the eight months before the coup, not included in the table, the parliament met 39 times, give or take one or two.
b. MacKintosh (1963: 339); and Nigeria House of Reps. (1960-65); and *West African Pilot* (1965-66). The Nigerian data are based on calendar years, so that 1959-60 is actually 1960. In the month of the coup, not included above, the parliament met three times.
c. Tanzania Natl. Assembly (1961-70) and William Tordoff (1965: 88). These data were calculated for 12-month periods, beginning on independence day, December 9, 1961.
d. *Uganda Argus* (1970-71) and Uganda Natl. Assembly (1962-70). Years are 12-month periods, beginning with independence, October 9, 1962. The parliament met 13 times from October 9, 1970, to the coup, January 25, 1971.
e. Kenya Natl. Assembly (1963-70). The figures are based on 12-month periods, beginning with independence, December 12, 1963.
f. Malawi Parl. (1964-71). Years dated from independence, July 6, 1964.
g. Zambia Natl. Assembly (1964-70). Years begin with data of independence, October 24, 1964.

where the functions of some of the organs of the ruling Tanganyika African National Union (TANU), especially the National Executive Committee, correspond very closely to those of the parliament (Bienen, 1970). The data on average number of days per year on which parliaments have been in session does help to assess the salience of these institutions within particular states (relatively low in Nigeria and Tanzania, and relatively high in Kenya, Uganda and Ghana), but they do not serve as indicators of regime stability.

The data become more interesting when we look at trends in parliamentary activity within the individual countries rather than simply at the average number of meetings. One obvious feature of parliamentary activity is that the annual averages of meetings are very erratic. (See crosses on Figures 1-7). There are many cases when the number of parliamentary meetings fell sharply. In Uganda meetings dropped 49 percent in 1967-68 and 30 percent in 1965-66 from the previous years. In Zambia parliamentary meetings dropped 42 percent in 1966-67, and in Kenya the decrease for 1968-69 was 35 percent.

In some, though not in all cases, these dramatic drops in parliamentary activity have coincided with periods of political turmoil and crisis. For instance, in February and March of 1966 the Prime Minister of Uganda, Milton Obote, suspended the constitution, had five cabinet ministers arrested at a cabinet meeting, and relieved the head of state, Sir Edward Mutesa (who was also the Kabak of Buganda), of the presidency. By late May the constitution had been rewritten, a centralized system of government substituted for a federal form, public protests launched by Baganda, and several hundred lives lost in fighting between the Army and Baganda at the Kabaka's palace. During most of this period, parliamentary government was inoperative, and where the regime was considered illegitimate compliance was obtained by force (Young, 1966). The crisis in Kenya in 1969 was less intense, but during the year the ruling party's Secretary-General, Tom Mboya, was assassinated; stones were thrown at the limousine of President Jomo Kenyatta; police fired on a crowd in Nyanza, killing at least nine people; and all opposition members of parliament were detained (Hakes, 1970). Throughout these events, parliament was meeting frequently compared to other African parliaments, but infrequently by previous Kenyan standards.

It is during times of stress and crisis that the questions of regime legitimacy and the ability of legislatures to generate public support assume special significance. The stress to which a regime is subjected may

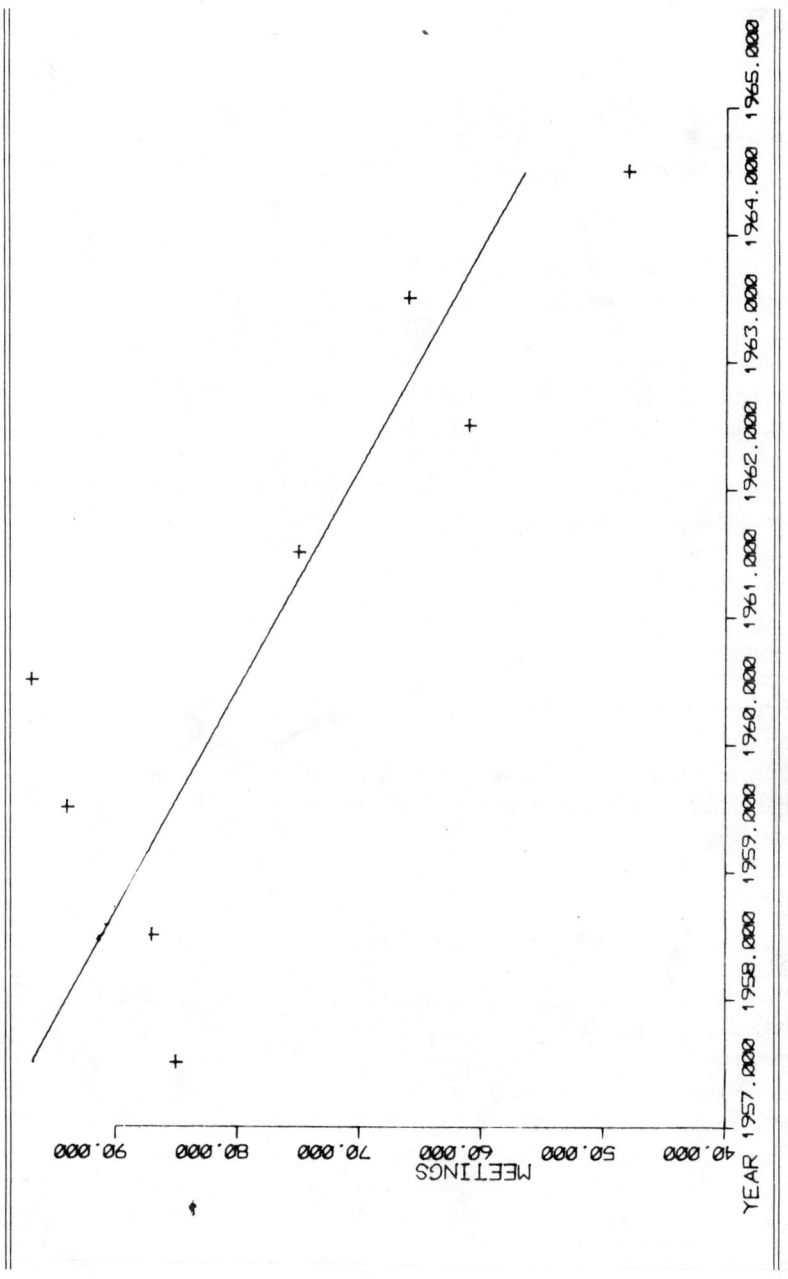

Figure 1. Parliamentary meetings in Ghana 1957-65

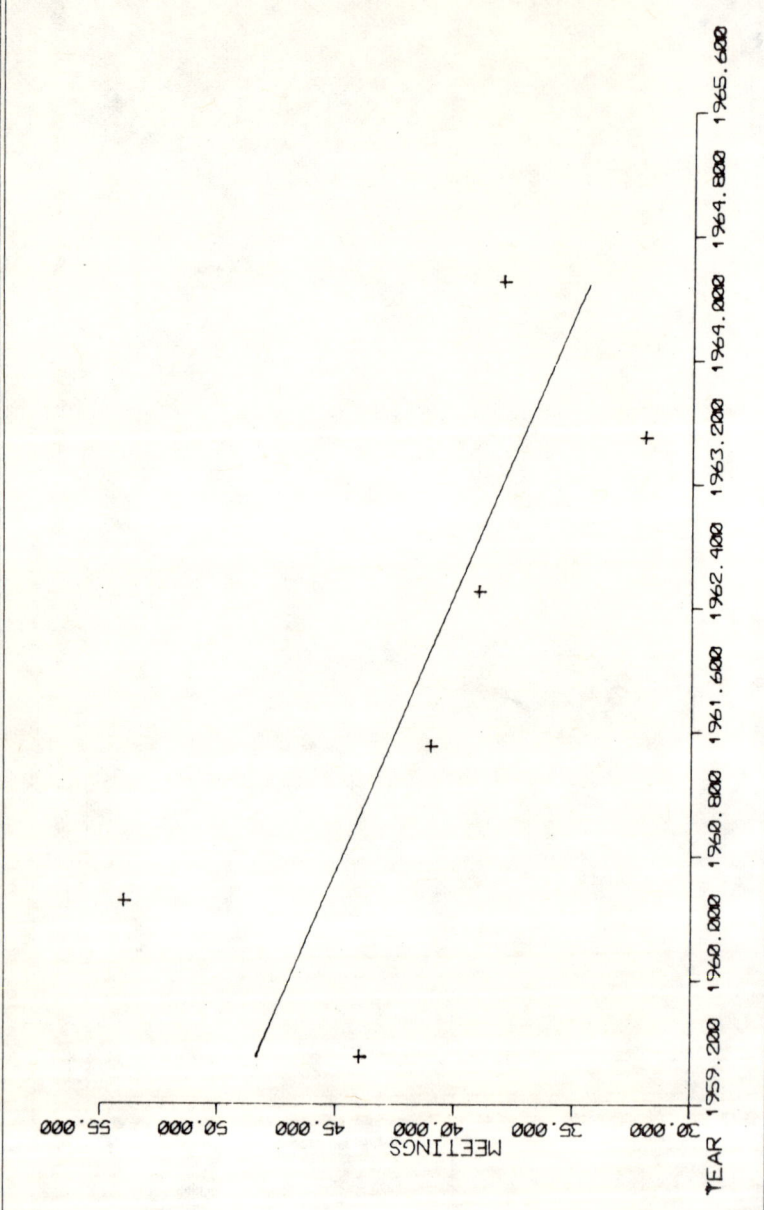

Figure 2. Parliamentary meetings in Nigeria 1959-65

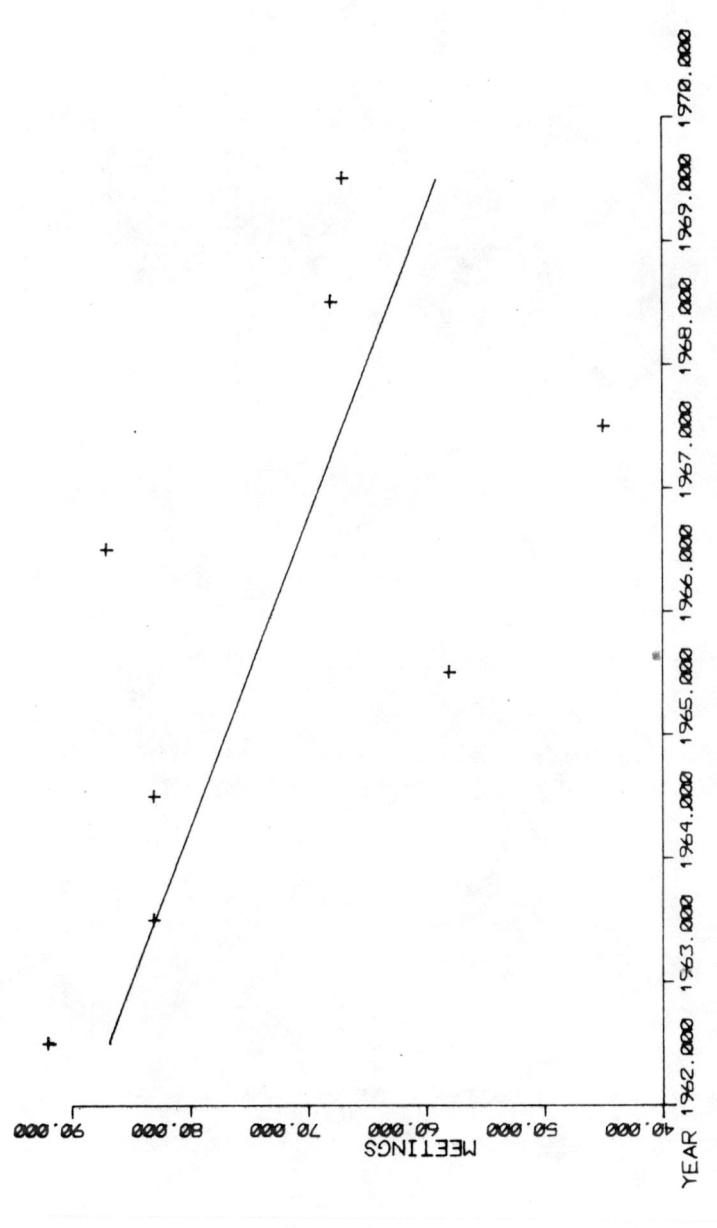

Figure 3. Parliamentary meetings in Uganda 1962-70

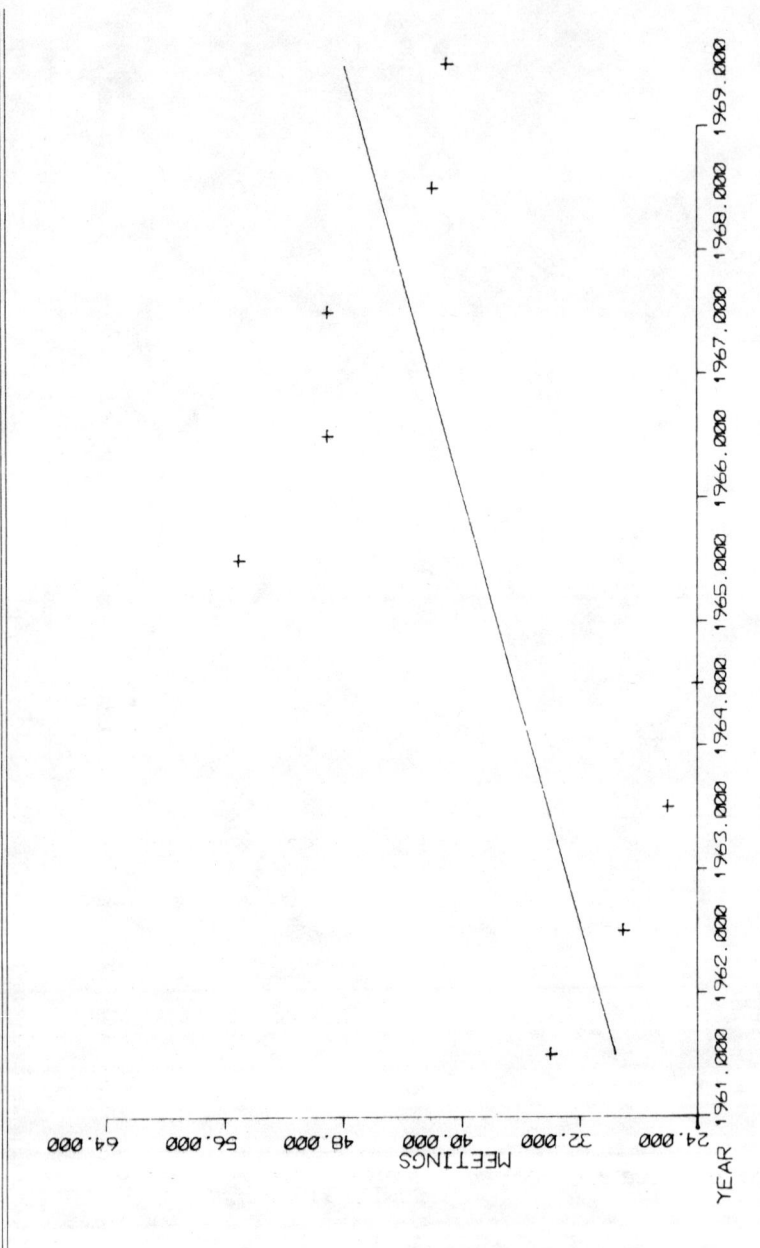

Figure 4. Parliamentary meetings in Tanzania 1961-70

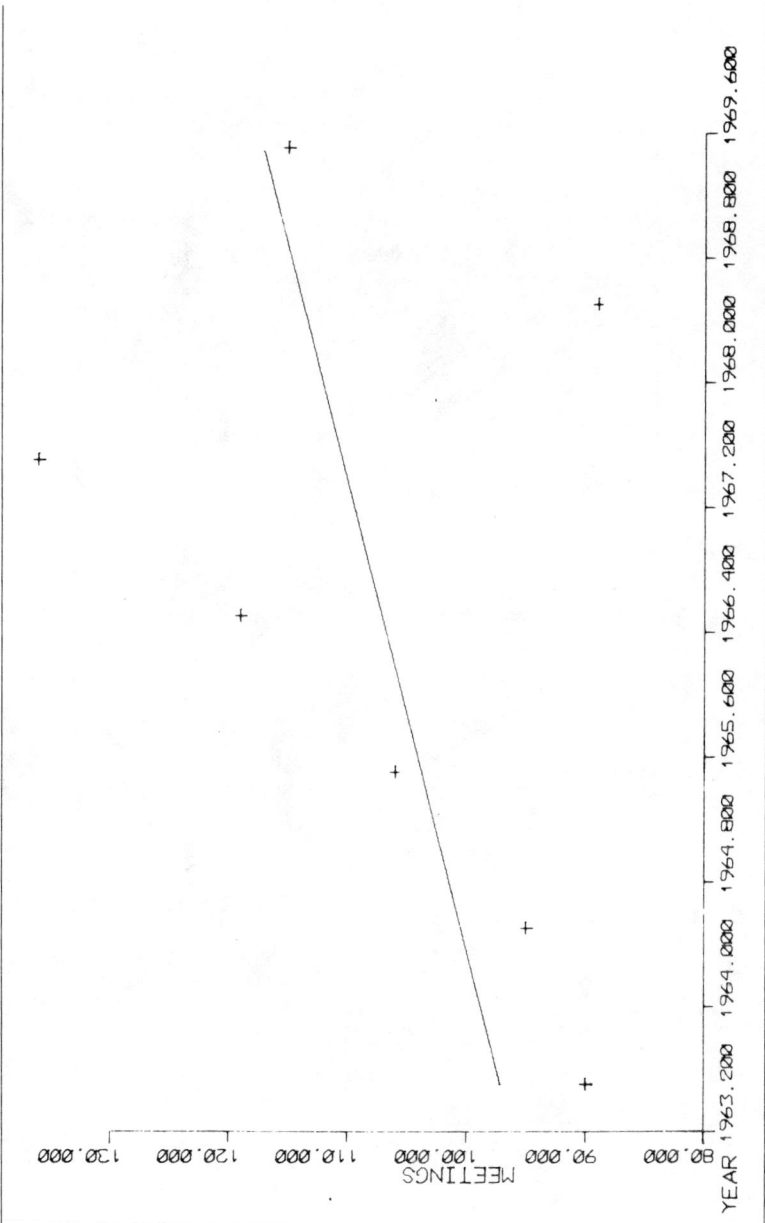

Figure 5. Parliamentary meetings in Kenya 1963-70

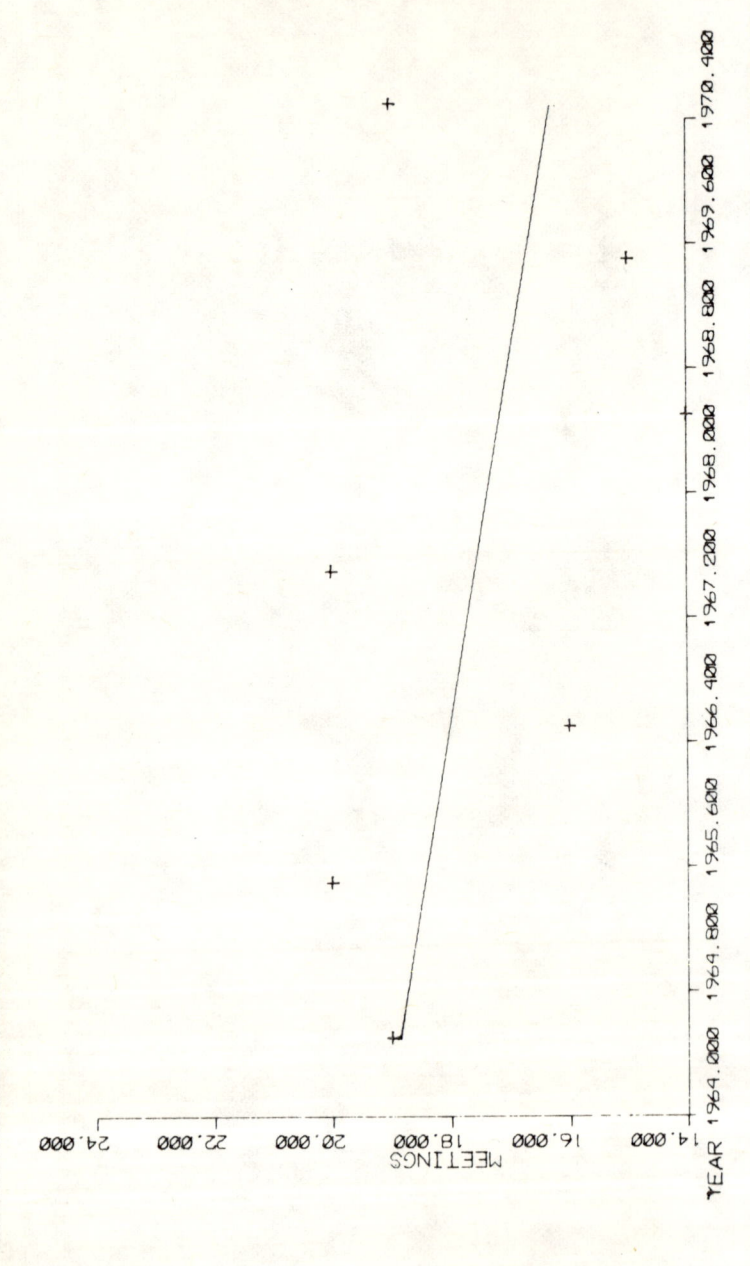

Figure 6. *Parliamentary meetings in Malawi 1964-71*

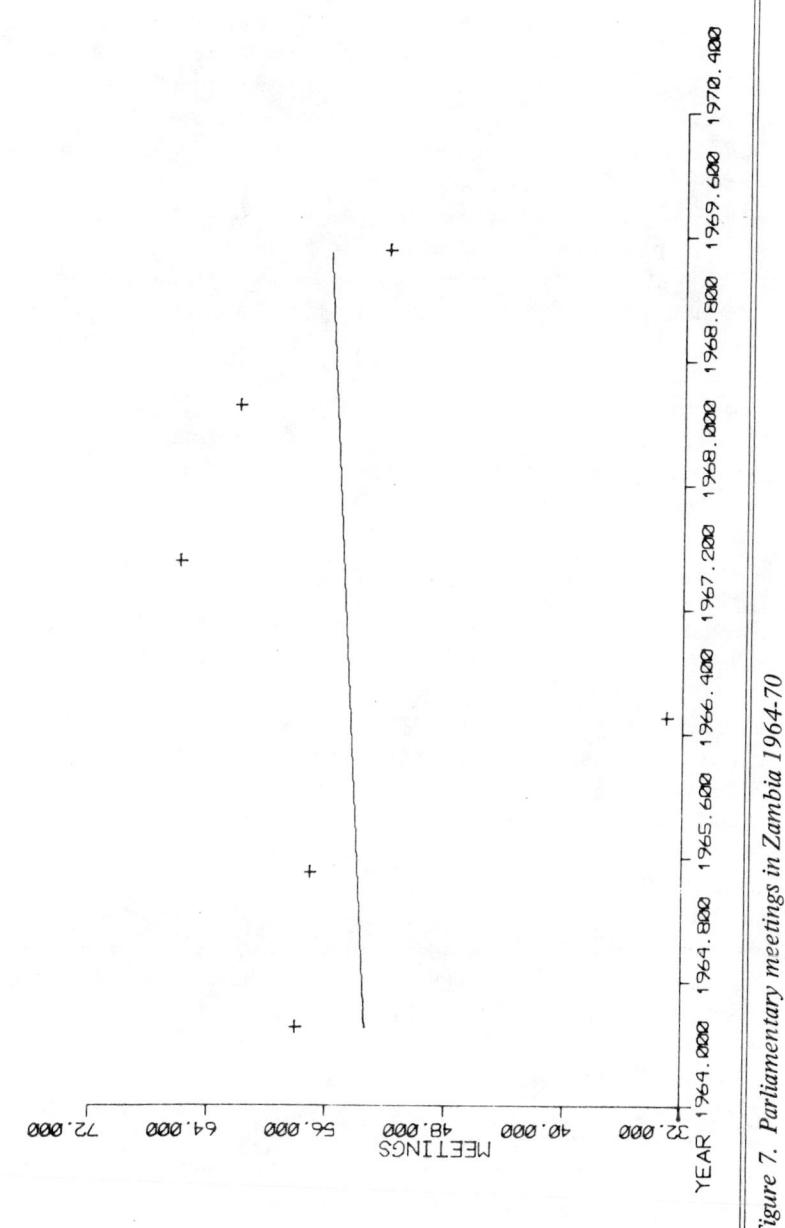

Figure 7. Parliamentary meetings in Zambia 1964-70

be the key for explaining regime instability, but the resopnse of political institutions must also be taken into account. In the African nations under consideration the meeting of parliament on a regular basis cannot be assumed. At times, the visibility of the institution has decreased sharply, and this situation might reasonably be expected to increase the vulnerability of a regime to loss of legitimacy and to instability.

Although the trends in parliamentary activity are erratic, the overall pattern is for the annual number of parliamentary meetings to decline in states where coups eventually occur and to increase in states where coups have not yet taken place. (See trend lines plotted on Figures 1-7). During the second three years of independence in Ghana, 1960-63, the National Assembly met 12 pecent less than during the first three years, 1957-60, and the decline continued up to the coup early in 1966. The pattern is similar in Nigeria, where the parliament met 22 percent less oftenduring the second three years than during the first three, and in Uganda, where parliamentary activity decreased 26 percent during the comparable periods. By contrast, in Tanzania the number of parliamentary meetings rose 44 percent from the first to the second three years. The increase for Zambia was 22 percent, and in Kenya it was 18 percent. Malawi, with an 11 percent drop during comparable periods but which has not had a coup, is an exception to the general pattern, but its rate of decrease in parliamentary activity is smaller than that of the states that have experienced coups.

The data seem to suggest that the absolute number of meetings of a parliament may not be as important as increases and decreases in the number of meetings. For example, the 55 meetings of the Tanzanian Bunge in 1965-66 may be more adequate in generating public support than the 58 meetings of the Uganda National Assembly in the same year. In Tanzania the organs of the ruling party shared the legitimating function more effectively with the legislature, and 55 meetings represented an increase of 129 percent over the previous year. In Uganda there had been greater dependence on the legislature for legitimacy, and the 58 meetings was the equivalent of a drop of 30 percent from the previous year. The sharp declines in parliamentary activity seem to have resulted form factors outside the legislature, such as crises produced by ethnic tension and the government's lack of self confidence. Thus, the decline in regime legitimacy should be seen as part of a complex of variables, of which decline in the saliency of the legislature is but one. Still, the destabilizing factors in the political system seem to affect legislative performance before the situation becomes serious enough for a coup to occur.

ACCOUNTABILITY AND ELECTIONS

Institutional salience, defined by the regularity and number of meetings, is one aspect of legislative capabilities for generating public support. Another is the extent to which legislatures are accountable to the public. A vital part of legislative accountability is the electoral process, which is inevitably intertwined with the properties of legislature, discussed earlier, that enable them to promote regime legitimacy. Because their authority derives from constitutions and regime norms, albeit imported, the activity of legislatures can symbolize the constitutional operation of governments. But legislatures cannot conform to regime norms unless their positions are filled by constitutional means, i.e., by elections at regular intervals. The second property of legislatures that enables them to perform a legitimizing function is their representativeness. Again, this characteristic of legislatures rests, in the Westminster style of government established in Anglophone Africa, on elections and voter choice.

Through the electoral process, legitimacy and support are given by the public in return for representation and consideration of its demands. At one level, this means that "legislative elections are means by which members of a significant part of the policy process receive voluntary commitments of support from followers, and the leadership in the legislature is empowered to follow general outlines of policy" (Milnor, 1969: 4). In this sense, elections perform a mobilizing function, if they create congruence, real or apparent, between the policies of elites and popular mandates. At another level, the electoral process may provide an opportunity for citizens to support not only specific candidates, but the political system as a whole. In this manner in particular, voting may contribute to the legitimacy of a regime.

As the African experience demonstrates, there is no guarantee that elections will produce a legislature chosen by the people. The problem is not so much with the powers of the executive to appoint members to parliament, since these involve only a small percentage of the total number of seats, as it is that the elections for constituency seats can be cancelled, postponed or rigged and that opposition candidates can be disallowed and intimidated by threats or the use of violence. On the other hand, elections can provide voters with genuine options and a fair opportunity to participate in the selection process. If the representativeness of legislatures (in the restricted sense of the term being used) can be utilized as an indicator of capability of generating support and for vulnerability to regime instability, we should expect to find a deterioration of the electoral process in states experiencing coups and a relatively stronger electoral process in states that have not yet experienced coups.

In Nigeria, Ghana and Uganda there is considerable evidence of deterioration of their electoral systems and the representativeness of their parliaments before the coups. In Nigeria, for instance, one major obstacle to public respect for the institution of parliament was the inability of the government to conduct an unrigged census, since the country's regions, which were dominated by ethnic hegemonies, began to inflate census reports to secure additional seats in the federal parliament. Without reliable census figures, it became impossible to apportion constituencies among the regions in a manner the populace considered fair. General elections had been held in 1959, one year before Nigerian independence, and the mandate of the parliament elected then was scheduled to run out after five years, as has been the case in other Commonwealth states. The elections were held in December of 1964 in three of Nigeria's four regions; polling in the Eastern Region took place early the following year. However, candidates ran unopposed in 78 of 310 constituencies, although in most cases potential opponents claimed that they had tried to run. The elections themselves were characterized by boycotts, rigging and even assassinations. This situation caused the Premier of the Eastern Region to declare the elections "a colossal farce—a daylight fraud" (Schwarz, 1968: 169). With significant sections of the population regarding the elections as a fraud, the position of the parliament as a representative structure was undermined. Events connected with attempts to elect the members of the Western Regional Assembly in 1965 suggested that future elections might deteriorate even further (Schwarz, 1968: 178-180).

Although Ghana, like Nigeria, began independence with a requirement of general elections at least every five years, those of June 9, 1965, were the first since 1956. The government of the Convention People's Party (CPP) regarded referenda in 1960 approving a new republican constitution and the election of Kwame Nkrumah as Ghana's first president as sufficient mandate for the continuation of its rule. During the nine-year interim, 34 by-elections were held, including ten necessitated by the detention of members of parliament. In the 1965 elections there was no opposition to the 198 CPP candiates. In fact, the public did not ever actually cast any ballots, since the nomination process did not involve them. The new National Assembly was very representative in the sense that its members were drawn from many diverse groups. In another sense, however, it was unrepresentative, since the voters had no direct influence on the selection of its members and since the members could not speak out on behalf of their groups because of the stringent requirements of party discipline (Kraus, 1965). The changes in the Ghanaian political system may have increased the capabilities of the party for generating popular support, but they certainly undermined the role of the National Assembly in this regard.

In Uganda general elections were held early in 1962, about half a year prior to independence. Although no single party won a majority of the seats, the Uganda People's Congress (UPC) became, first by means of coalition and later because of massive crossing of the floor by opposition members, the dominant party in the National Assembly. The strength of the UPC in parliament was deceptive, because disputes over the rights and interest of traditional kingdoms were serious obstacles to national unity and led directly to the turmoil of 1966 discussed earlier. At the time of the coup, January 25, 1971, no general elections had been held since 1962, although they had been promised by April of 1971 under a new electoral formula. In addition, no by-elections were held after the state of virtual civil war in 1966, so that by the time of the coup 20 of the 92 seats in the National Assembly were vacant, leaving more than a fifth of the population without any formal representation in parliament (Uganda Natl. Assembly, 1966-70 and *Uganda Argus*, 1970).

In each of the countries where coups have occurred, the ability of the populace to participate in the selection of its legislators was severly limited or non-existent at the time the civilian regimes were overturned. The breakdowns of electoral processes occurred over a period of time. Voters had at one point experienced participation in the selection of legislators, and this experience increased their frustration when their privileges were later constricted. None of the coups occurred before the first five-year mandates of the parliaments had expired or before trends of decreasing popular participation in selecting legislators had become clear. These cases in no way suggest that failures in the electoral process "cause" military coups. Several factors, particularly communal conflicts, seem to have led to both decay of the electoral process and the eventual decision of the military to intervene. The cases do suggest, however, that during the periods preceding coups public accountability of legislatures and, we might deduce, the legitimacy of the regime were in a state of decline.

Electoral systems in Tanzania, Kenya and Zambia have provided for more popular participation in selecting parliamentarians than have those in Nigeria, Ghana and Uganda. Moreover, trends of overall decline in popular participation have generally not been evident in the noncoup states. Tanzania's pre-independence elections of 1960, for instance, were followed by elections in 1965 and 1970, in keeping with requirements for elections at least every five years. Tanzania is the only one of our seven countries that has held two general elections after independence. Moreover, the polling after independence has offered voters more genuine options than did previous elections. In 1960 TANU won 70 of 71 seats in the (then) Legislative Council; the only non-TANU winner was an independent whose TANU candidacy had been vetoed by national party headquarters (Bienen, 1970: 55-56). TANU's dominance did not result from governmental interference; the colonial administration in power was not pro-TANU. Instead, the party's victory can be attributed to its nationwide popularity and superior organization. Rather than simply presenting another slate of TANU candidates to be ratified by the voters in 1965, the TANU leadership chose to implement a single party electoral system in which most voters would have a choice between two TANU candidates. In the one party elections of 1965 two cabinet ministers and six junior ministers were defeated, and less than a quarter of the sitting MPs were able to secure reelection (Cliffe, 1967: 300 and Tordoff, 1967: 39). The one party system was used again in 1970, although the turnover of MPs was not as great, and it has clearly increased the impact of popular participation. Popular participation in the selection of legislators, however, has been limited to the mainland sections of Tanzania (Tanganyika); the 23 MPs from the island of Zanzibar are appointed by the Zanzibar Revolutionary Council. On the mainland President Nyerere can appoint a few members of parliamant but the main limitation on the ability of the electorate to choose its legislators has been the preventive detention of several MPs.

In Kenya the electoral picture has been complicated. Preindependence elections were held in May of 1963, about half a year before independence. Somali boycotts in the Northeastern Region preventing the filling of five of the 117 constituency seats in the House of Representatives, and the last of these vacant seats was not filled until late in 1964. Another general election was not held within five years of the 1963 ballotting because of the amalgamation of the House of Representatives and the Senate. Some Senators had been elected for six-year terms as late as 1965, and the extension of the life of parliament was an inducement to the Senators to go along with the merger. The postponed elections were eventually held in December of 1969, but the role the public would be allowed to play was at first unclear. The local government elections of 1967 had been rigged, and the MPs in the opposition Kenya People's Union (KPU) were detained in October of 1969. Nonetheless, the one-party elections in December provided considerable choice for the voters, as almost 600 candidates ran in 159 constituencies. Some critics of the government were elected and five ministers, 16 assistant ministers and about two thirds of the backbenchers were not re-elected. The elections provided the parliament with a new five-year mandate in which the public had been permitted to exercise considerable choice (Hakes, 1970).

Zambia's first general elections after independence were held in December 1968, before the five-year term of the old parliament had expired. The extent of the Zambian voter's options depended on the freedom of opposition parties to run candidates, and the attitude of the government on this issue was ambivalent. With regard to the opposition United Party, "U.N.I.P. (the ruling United National Independence Party) has relied heavily upon tactics of coercion, harassment, and intimidation, culminating in the banning of U.P. in August 1968" (Rasmussen, 1969: 407-408). However, not all opposition was banned. Ian Scott and Robert Molteno (1969: 42) have said of the 1968 ballotting:

> In an election made as fair as possible by scrupulous electoral administration. . ., UNIP increased its share of the popular vote and its representation in the enlarged National Assembly. But at the same time, in an unexpected turn, Harry Nkumbula's opposition African National Congress. . .almost tripled its parliamentary representation and unseated some prominent members of the government.

The election, then, preserved a large measure of popular participation in the selection of Zambian legislators although Zambia has since become a one-party state.

The electoral history of Malawi is highly unusual. The elections of 1964, scheduled to lead to independence the following year, were never held, because no opposition candidates filed nomination papers. Consequently, the 50 candidates of the Malawi Congress Party were elected unopposed (Sanger, 1964). Malawi's first elections after independence were held in April of 1971. According to James Hooker (1971: 1), "Almost no one outside the country seemed aware of (the elections): indeed, many inside this landlocked republic are just as poorly informed." The candidates of the Malawi Congress Party were personally selected by President Hastings Banda and, again, all were returned unopposed. No popular involvement in the selection of the legislature took place, but no downward trend is evident because of the similarities between events in 1964 and 1971.

The ability of the public to participate in elections involves many factors, but the existence or absence of opposition parties does not seem to have been a very important one. Public choice can be provided either by opposition parties or by primary elections within a single party. Although the ritual act of voting may help to provide support for a regime, statistics on voter turnout may not indicate very accurately the effectiveness of particular elections in legitimizing a regime, since voting may be coerced and since information on turnout supplied by government officials may not always be credible. Another aspect of the electoral process, voter choice, can be more easily operationalized. Unless the voters can in some way render a verdict with his ballot, the electoral process itself can hardly contribute to the representative nature of the legislature. The measure of voter choice is whether or not constituencies are contested. Such an index can be based on reliable information and seems closely related to the functional aspect of elections in which we are particularly interested.

Table 4 shows that in each of the countries where coups have occurred either general elections were never held after independence (Uganda) or if held they involved fewer contested seats than did the last elections before independence (Ghana and Nigeria). In the countries where coups have not occurred either more seats were contested after than before independence (Tanzania, Kenya, and Zambia) or there is no change (Malawi). In the case of Tanzania the trend upward is dramatic. If public support for legislatures is exchanged for popular participation in the selection of legislators, support for legislative institutions should have declinded in Ghana, Nigera and Uganda and increased in Tanzania, Kenya, and Zambia.

The purpose of this analysis of popular participation in the selection of legislators is not to assess the absolute levels of democracy in these seven states. As was the case with our study of institutional salience, emphasis has been placed on the trends within individual countries. One country may need less popular participation than another to maintain the legitimacy of its regime; this situation suggests that other variables (e.g., the size of the elite placing demands on the system, which may explain Malawi's stability despite a lack of competitive elections) might at some

Table 4. Constituencies with more than one candidate in national elections before and after independence in Anglophone Africa

Nations with Coups	Last National Election before Independence	First National Election after Independence
Ghana[a]	95%	0%
(1956 & 1965)		
Nigeria[b]	100	75
(1959 & 1964)		
Uganda[c]	92	—
(1962)		
Nations without Coups		
Tanzania[d]	18	94
(1960 & 1965)		
Kenya[e]	84	96
(1963 & 1969)		
Malawi[f]	0	0
(1964 & 1971)		
Zambia[g]	68	71
(1964 & 1968)		

a. *The Times* (1956) and Kraus (1965).
b. Post (1963: 451-74) and Schwarz (1968: 166-68).
c. *The Times* (1961). The 21 seats in Buganda were filled by the Buganda Regional Assembly.
d. Bienen (1970: 55, 387). The figures are for the mainland only.
e. Sanger and Nottingham (1964: 34) and *East African Standard* (1969).
f. Sanger (1964) and Hooker (1971)
g. Mulford (1964) and Scarritt (1969).

point be added to the analysis. However, it seems clear that in each country the public has been led to expect a certain level of choice in the electoral process and that when expectations are frustrated public support for legislatures declines.

The case for using an index of popular participation based on percentage of contested seats is strengthened by its relationship with our index of institutional saliency based on annual number of meetings. Nations with increasing institutional salience tend also to be characterized by

Table 5. Association between trends in parliamentary activity and competitiveness of elections

Nation	Parliamentary Meetings Annual % Change	% Change in Contested Constituencies
Tanzania	5.7	76
Kenya	4.1	12
Zambia	.8	3
Malawi	-4.5	0
Nigeria	-7.1	-25
Uganda	-6.1	-92
Ghana	-8.2	-95
	r = .90	

increasing popular participation; nations low on one index tend also to be low on the other (see Table 5). A Pearson's r of .90 suggests that the two indexes are closely related and probably reflect some overall attitude of the respective governments toward the importance of legislatures as legitimating institutions.

CONCLUSIONS

As Aristide Zolberg (1968a: 72) has said:

> Whether or not a major military intervention occurs in a given African country at a particular time is related to highly specific and circumstantial features of that country's current political situation, rather than to any basic deviant political characteristics.

However, the present study suggests that the political processes leading to military coups may not be entirely inscrutable. All political events retain a certain impenetrability, and military coups are not more subject to precise predictions than other political phenomena. On the otherhand, coups are not uniquely mysterious occurrences.

Vulnerability to military intervention is increased by the failure or decline of legitimating processes within states starting well before the day the military seizes power. In Anglophone Africa—where the legal and constitutional order provided parliaments with central roles in legitimation and where certain ideas about parliamentary government have been transmitted to the elites, including military officers—decreases in regime legitimacy have frequently been associated with declines in the capabilities of legislatures to generate popular support. It would appear that diminishing salience and public accountability were important factors in restricting parliamentary capabilities in this area. Outside of Anglophone Africa, a breakdown in the legitimating process might take on a different configuration, depending on the characteristics of particular systems.

Our study of Anglophone Africa has many limitations. One is the small number of cases. Unfortunately, the cases could not be selected randomly, since our study was confined to those states in Africa for which parliamentary debates are available. This criterion of selection introduces a bias, since the governments of states that regularly publish parliamentary debates could be assumed to attribute more importance to parliamentary institutions than those in states that do not publish these documents regularly. Thus, our findings do not have universal or even continental application. What we can say is that in states that ascribe importance to legislative bodies, as indicated by their publication of debates, the behavior of these institutions seems to be related to trends in the legitimacy of regimes.

A second limitation is the small number of variables we have been able to treat systematically. The data in Table 2, for instance, indicate that literacy and newspaper circulation might have utility as explanatory variables. Three of the four highest states on each indicator have had coups, while the lowest three have not. Perhaps expansion in literacy and communications has been a destabilizing force. Ethnic conflict is another factor in the politics of instability in Africa that we have not analyzed systematically. On the surface, ethnic conflict often appears to have been the prime stimulus of unstable conditions. Declines in the effectiveness of national political institutions do seem to have been encouraged by ethnic tension. On the other hand, however, ethnic loyalty has often been a response to growing cynicism about national political institutions. As data becomes increasingly available, we should look for patterns of reciprocal relationships rather than "first causes."

Despite the present crude stage of the analysis, we might venture the assessment that the prospects for regime stability are better in Tanzania than in Kenya, Zambia, or especially Malawi, the other three countries in our analysis that have not experienced coups. The Tanzanian parliament has met less frequently than other parliaments in Africa, but in 1965 it greatly increased its rate of activity and, hence, its salience for the public. In addition, Tanzania's parliament has met more regularly than other parliaments. Moreover, with two general elections having been held since independence, Tanzania is much further along than the other systems in institutionalizing the public accountability of its legislators. As a result, the regime's aura of legitimacy remains relatively intact.

NOTES

1. The importance of legislatures in generating public support for regimes has frequently been noted in studies of Western systems. For two recent examples, see Patterson et al. (1973) and Loewenberg (1971).

2. For evidence that former colonial powers have played decisive roles in determining whether or not civilian regimes in Africa fall, see First (1972: 423-424) and Zolberg (1973: 325-327).

3. Studies of military intervention outside Africa have tended to support the position of Finer (1962: 21) that "where public attachment to civilian institutions is strong, military intervention in politics will be weak. . . . Where public attachment to civilian institutions is weak or non-existent, military intervention in politics will find wide scope." See Johnson (1962: 127) and Putnam (1967: 85-86).

4. For a review of literature on parliaments in Anglophone Africa, see Stultz (1968). For more recent studies of these legislatures, see Hopkins (1970) and Hakes and Helgerson (1973).

5. Exceptions to these trends have appeared. Zolberg (1966) was an important stimulus to the realistic study of African politics. See also Bretton (1966).

6. A number of factors affect the reliability of data on Africa. First, the data in their original form often constitute at best rough estimates. This objection applies to almost all kinds of census data. Second, it is almost impossible to code precisely factory such as ethnicity or elite and communal stability. Third, the use of large research teams tends to diffuse responsibility and sometimes permits data to be reported inaccurately. The author is willing to supply by personal communications documentation of faulty reporting of data.

7. The author has inspected collections of parliamentary records at these libraries: Members' Library of the Kenya National Assembly, The Library of Congress, and libraries at the following universities, Nairobi, Dar es Salaam, Makerere, Duke, Harvard, Boston, and Northwestern. Several of these libraries possess virtually complete collections of parliamentary debates from Anglophone Africa; Cartwright (1970: 284) has reported that publication of *Parliamentary Debates* in Sierra Leone ceased from 1959 to 1962. Hansards were also available for many national assemblies in Francophone Africa, but none of the sets were complete. Libraries in English-speaking countries would be expected to have a bias in favor of materials from other English-speaking states, but the impression was left that the Francophone parliaments have, in many cases, not publsihed their debates regularly.

REFERENCES

BIENEN, H. (1970) Tanzania: Party Transformation and Economic Development, rev. ed. Princeton: Princeton University Press.

BOYNTON, G. R., S. C. PATTERSON, and R. D. HEDLUND (1969) "The missing link in legislative politics: attentive constituents." J. of Politics 31 (August): 700-702.

BRETTON, H. (1966) The Rise and Fall of Kwame Nkrumah. New York: Praeger.

CARTWRIGHT, J. R. (1970) Politics in Sierra Leone, 1947-1967. Toronto: University of Toronto Press.

CLIFFE, L. (1967) "Factors and issues," pp. 299-327 in Cliffe (ed.) One Party Democracy: The 1965 Tanzania General Elections. Nairobi: East African Publishing House.

CROW, R. E. (1970) "Parliament in the Lebanese political system," pp. 273-302 in A. Kornberg and L. Musolf (eds.) Legislatures in Developmental Perspective. Durham, N.C.: Duke University Press.

EASTON, D. (1965) A Systems Analysis of Political Life. New York: John Wiley.

FINER, S. E. (1962) The Man on Horseback: The Role of the Military in Politics. New York: Praeger.

FIRST, R. (1972) Power in Africa: Political Power in Africa and the Coup d'Etat. Baltimore: Penguin Books.

Ghana National Assembly (1957-1965) Parliamentary Debates. Accra: Government Printer.

GUTTERIDGE, W. (1972) "Opportunism and military interventions in black Africa." East Africa Journal 9 (September): 8-18.

HAKES, J. E. (1970) "Election year politics in Kenya." Current History 58 (March): 154-159, 177.

HAKES, J. E. and J. L. HELGERSON (1973) "Bargaining and parliamentary behavior in Africa: a comparative study of national assemblies in Zambia and Kenya," pp. 335-362 in A. Kornberg (ed.) Legislatures in Comparative Perspective. New York: David McKay.

HOOKER, J. (1971) "Malawi's general election." American Universities Fieldstaff Reports, Central & Southern Africa Series 15 (June): 1-6.

HOPKINS, R. F. (1970) "The role of the M.P. in Tanzania." Amer. Pol. Sci. Rev. 64 (September): 754-771.

JOHNSON, J. J. (1962) "The Latin American military as a politically competing group in transitional societies," pp. 91-129 in J. J. Johnson (ed.) The Role of the Military in Underdeveloped Countries. Princeton: Princeton University Press.

Kenya National Assembly (1963-1970) Reports. Nairobi: Government Printer.

KRAUS, J. (1965) "Ghana's new 'corporate parliament'." Africa Report 10 (August): 6-11.

LEE, J. M. (1963) "Parliament in republican Ghana." Parliamentary Affairs 16 (Autumn): 376-395.

LERNER, D. (1958) The Passing of Traditional Society. New York: The Free Press.

LOEWENBERG, G. (1971) "The influence of parliamentary behavior on regime stability: some conceptual clarifications." Comparative Politics 3 (January): 177-200.

MACKINTOSH, J. P. (1963) "The Nigerian Federal Parliament." Public Law 8 (Autumn): 333-361.
Malawi Parliament (1964-1971) Debates, Zomba: Government Printer.
MILNOR, A. J. (1969) Elections and Political Stability. Boston: Little, Brown.
MORRISON, D. G., R. C. MITCHELL, J. N. PADEN, and H. M. STEVENSON (1972) Black Africa: A Comparative Handbook. New York: The Free Press.
MULFORD, D. C. (1964) "Northern Rhodesia: some observations on the 1964 elections." Africa Report 9 (February): 13-17.
Nigeria House of Representatives (1960-1965) Parliamentary Debates. Lagos: Government Printer.
PACKENHAM, R. A. (1979) "Legislatures and political development," pp. 521-582 in A. Kornberg and L. Musolf (eds.) Legislatures in Developmental Perspective. Durham, N.C.: Duke University Press.
PATTERSON, S.C., J. C. WAHLKE, and G. R. BOYNTON (1973) "Dimensions of support in legislative systems," pp. 282-313 in A. Kornberg (ed.) Legislatures in Comparative Perspective. New York: David McKay.
POST, K. W. J. (1963) The Nigerian Federal Election of 1959. London: Oxford University Press.
PUTNAM, R. D. (1967) "Toward explaining military intervention in Latin American politics." World Politics 20 (October): 83-110.
RASMUSSEN, T. (1969) "Political competition and one-party dominance in Zambia." J. of Modern African Studies 7 (October): 407-424.
SANGER, C. (1964) "Nyasaland becomes Malawi." Africa Report 9 (August): 8-11.
SANGER, C. and J. NOTTINGHAM (1964) "The Kenya election of 1963." J. of Modern African Studies 2 (March): 1-40.
SCARRITT, J. A. (1969) "The Zambian election–triumph or tragedy?" Africa Today 15 (February-March): 4-5.
SCHWARZ, W. (1968) Nigeria. New York: Frederick Praeger.
SCOTT, I. and R. MOLTENO (1969) "The Zambia general elections." Africa Report 14 (January): 42-47.
STULTZ, N. M. (1970) "The National Assembly in the politics of Kenya," pp. 303-333 in A. Kornberg and L. Musolf (eds.) Legislatures in Developmental Perspective. Durham, N.C.: Duke University Press.
——— (1968) "Parliaments in former British black Africa." J. of Developing Areas 2 (July): 479-494.
Tanzania National Assembly (1961-1970) Assembly Debates. Dar es Salaam: Government Printer.
TAYLOR, C. L. and M. C. HUDSON (1972) World Handbook of Political and Social Indicators, 2nd ed. New Haven: Yale University Press.
TORDOFF, W. (1965) "Parliament in Tanzania," J. of Commonwealth Political Studies 3 (July): 85-103.
——— (1967) Government and Politics in Tanzania. Nairobi: East African Publishing House.
Uganda National Assembly (1962-1970) Parliamentary Debates. Entebbe: Government Printer.

YOUNG, M. C. (1966) "The Obote revolution." Africa Report 11 (June): 8-14.
Zambia National Assembly (1964-1970) Debates. Lusaka: Government Printer.
ZOLBERG, A. R. (1973) "The military decade in Africa." World Politics 25 (January): 309-331.
--- (1968a) "Military intervention in the new states of tropical Africa: elements of comparative analysis," pp. 71-98 in H. Bienen (ed.) The Military Intervenes: Case Studies in Political Development. New York: Russell Sage Foundation.
--- (1968b) "The structure of Political conflict in the new states of Africa." Amer. Pol. Sci. Rev. 62 (March): 70-87.
--- (1966) Creating Political Order: The Party States of West Africa. Chicago: Rand McNally.

JAY E. HAKES is Associate Professor of Political Science at Louisiana State University in New Orleans. He studied the Kenya National Assembly in 1968-69 and has contributed articles to such edited volumes as Legislatures in Comparative Perspective, *and* Americana Annual, *as well as to the journal,* Current History.

A Better Way of Getting New Information

Research, survey and policy studies that say what needs to be said—
no more, no less.

The Sage Papers Program

Five regularly-issued original paperback series that bring, at an unusually low cost, the timely writings and findings of the international scholarly community. Since the material is updated on a continuing basis, each series rapidly becomes a unique repository of vital information.

Authoritative, and frequently seminal, works that NEED to be available

- To scholars and practitioners
- In university and institutional libraries
- In departmental collections
- For classroom adoption

Sage Professional Papers
COMPARATIVE POLITICS SERIES
INTERNATIONAL STUDIES SERIES
ADMINISTRATIVE AND POLICY STUDIES SERIES
AMERICAN POLITICS SERIES

Sage Policy Papers
THE WASHINGTON PAPERS

SAGE PUBLICATIONS
The Publishers of Professional Social Science
Beverly Hills • London

Sage Professional Papers in **Comparative Politics**

Editors: **Harry Eckstein,** *Princeton University,* **Ted Robert Gurr,** *Northwestern University,* and **Aristide R. Zolberg,** *University of Chicago.*

VOLUME 1 (1970)

- 01-001 **J.Z. Namenwirth & H. D. Lasswell,** The changing language of American values: a computer study of selected party platforms $2.50/£1.05
- 01-002 **K. Janda,** A conceptual framework for the comparative analysis of political parties $1.90/£.80
- 01-003 **K. Thompson,** Cross-national voting behavior research $1.50/£.60
- 01-004 **W. B. Quandt,** The comparative study of political elites $2.00/£.85
- 01-005 **M. C. Hudson,** Conditions of political violence and instability $1.90/£.80
- 01-006 **E. Ozbudun,** Party cohesion in western democracies $3.00/£1.30
- 01-007 **J. R. Nellis,** A model of developmental ideology in Africa $1.40/£.55
- 01-008 **A. Kornberg,** et al., Semi-careers in political organizations $1.40/£.55
- 01-009 **F. I. Greenstein & S. Tarrow,** Political orientations of children $2.90/£1.25
- 01-010 **F. W. Riggs,** Administrative reform and political responsiveness: a theory of dynamic balance $1.50/£.60
- 01-011 **R. H. Donaldson & D. J. Waller,** Stasis and change in revolutionary elites: a comparative analysis of the 1956 Central Party Committees in China and the USSR $1.90/£.80
- 01-012 **R. A. Pride,** Origins of democracy: a cross-national study of mobilization, party systems and democratic stability $2.90/£1.25

VOLUME II (1971)

- 01-013 **S. Verba,** et al., The modes of democratic participation $2.80/£1.20
- 01-014 **W. R. Schonfeld,** Youth and authority in France $2.80/£1.20
- 01-015 **S. J. Bodenheimer,** The ideology of developmentalism $2.40/£1.00
- 01-016 **L. Sigelman,** Modernization and the political system $2.50/£1.05
- 01-017 **H. Eckstein,** The evaluation of political performance: problems and dimensions $2.90/£1.25
- 01-018 **T. Gurr & M. McLelland,** Political performance: a twelve nation study $2.90/£1.25
- 01-019 **R. F. Moy,** A computer simulation of democratic political development $2.70/£1.15
- 01-020 **T. Nardin,** Violence and the state $2.70/£1.15
- 01-021 **W. Ilchman,** Comparative public administration and "conventional wisdom" $2.40/£1.00
- 01-022 **G. Bertsch,** Nation-building in Yugoslavia $2.25/£.95
- 01-023 **R. J. Willey,** Democracy in West German trade unions $2.40/£1.00
- 01-024 **R. Rogowski & L. Wasserspring,** Does political development exist? Corporatism in old and new societies $2.40/£1.00

VOLUME III (1972)

- 01-025 **W. T. Daly,** The revolutionary $2.10/£.90
- 01-026 **C. Stone,** Stratification and political change in Trinidad and Jamaica $2.10/£.90
- 01-027 **Z. Y. Gitelman,** The diffusion of political innovation: from Eastern Europe to the Soviet Union $2.50/£1.05
- 01-028 **D. P. Conradt,** The West German party system $2.40/£1.00
- 01-029 **J. R. Scarritt,** Political development and culture change theory [Africa] $2.50/£1.05
- 01-030 **M. D. Hayes,** Policy outputs in the Brazilian states $2.25/£.95
- 01-031 **B. Stallings,** Economic dependency in Africa and Latin America $2.50/£1.05
- 01-032 **J. T. Campos & J. F. McCamant,** Cleavage shift in Colombia: analysis of the 1970 elections $2.90/£1.25
- 01-033 **G. Field & J. Higley,** Elites in developed societies [Norway] $2.25/£.95
- 01-034 **J. S. Szyliowicz,** A political analysis of student activism [Turkey] $2.80/£1.20
- 01-035 **E. C. Hargrove,** Professional roles in society and government [England] $2.90/£1.25
- 01-036 **A. J. Sofranko & R. J. Bealer,** Unbalanced modernization and domestic instability $2.90/£1.25

VOLUME IV (1973)

- 01-037 **W. A. Cornelius,** Political learning among the migrant poor $2.90/£1.25
- 01-038 **J. W. White,** Political implications of cityward migration [Japan] $2.50/£1.05
- 01-039 **R. B. Stauffer,** Nation-building in a global economy: the role of the multi-national corporation $2.25/£.95
- 01-040 **A. Martin,** The politics of economic policy in the U.S. $2.50/£1.05

Forthcoming, summer/fall 1973

- 01-041 **M. B. Welfling,** Political Institutionalization [African party systems] $2.70*/£1.15
- 01-042 **B. Ames,** Rhetoric and reality in a militarized regime [Brazil] $2.40*/£1.00
- 01-043 **E. C. Browne,** Coalition theories $2.90*/£1.25
- 01-044 **M. Barrera,** Information and ideology: a study of Arturo Frondizi $2.40*/£1.00

*denotes tentative price

Papers 01-045 through 01-048 to be announced

Sage Professional Papers

Editor: Vincent Davis *and* Mau...

VOLUME I (1972)

- 02-001 **E. E. Azar,** et al., Int...
  events interaction an...
  $2.80/£1.20
- 02-002 **J. H. Sigler,** et al., A...
  events data analysis
- 02-003 **J. C. Burt,** Decision...
  the world population
  $2.25/£.95
- 02-004 **J. A. Caporaso,** Func...
  regional integration
- 02-005 **E. R. Wittkopf,** West...
  aid allocations $2.5...
- 02-006 **T. L. Brewer,** Foreig...
  tions: American elite
  variations in threat, t...
  surprise $2.50/£1.0...
- 02-007 **W. F. Weiker,** Decent...
  ernment in moderniz...
  [Turkish provinces]
- 02-008 **F. A. Beer,** The polit...
  of alliances: benefits,
  institutions in NATO
- 02-009 **C. Mesa-Lago.** The la...
  employment, unemp...
  underemployment in
  1970 $2.70/£1.15
- 02-010 **P. M. Burgess & R. W...**
  cators of internation...
  an assessment of ever...
  research $3.00/£1....
- 02-011 **W. Minter,** Imperial...
  external dependency
  $2.70/£1.15

Sage Professional Papers i...

Administra...

Editor: H. George Frederickso...

VOLUME I (1973)

- 03-001 **E. Ostrom, W. Baug...**
  R. Parks, G. Whitak...
  organization and th...
  police services $3...
- 03-002 **R. S. Ahlbrandt, Jr.**
  protection services
- 03-003 **D. O. Porter with D...**
  T. W. Porter. The p...
  ing federal aid [loca...
  $3.00/£1.30
- 03-004 **J. P. Viteritti,** Polic...
  pluralism in New Y...
  $2.70/£1.15

The 1973 summer/fall papers...
- 03-005 **R. L. Schott,** Profes...
  service: characteristi...
  tion of engineer fed...

ORDER FORM

name _____

institution _____

address _____

city/state/zip _____

Please enter subscription(s) to:

- ☐ Prof. Pprs. in Administrative & Policy Studies
- ☐ Prof. Pprs. in Comparative Politics
- ☐ Prof. Pprs. in American Politics
- ☐ Prof. Pprs. in International Studies
- ☐ The Washington Papers

Please send the individual papers whose numbers I have listed below:

_____
_____
_____

- ☐ Please invoice (INSTITUTIONS ONLY) quoting P.O. # _____ (shipping and handling additional on non-subscription orders)
- ☐ Payment enclosed (Sage pays shipping charges)

INSTITUTIONAL ORDERS FOR LESS THAN $10.00 AND *ALL* PERSONAL ORDERS *MUST BE PREPAID*. (California residents: please add 6% sales tax on non-subscription orders.)

MAIL TO:

 SAGE Publications, Inc. / P.O. Box 5024 Beverly Hills, California 90210

orders from the U.K., Europe, the Middle East and Africa should be sent to Sage Publications, Ltd, 44 Hatton Garden, London EC1N 8ER

A Sage Policy Papers Series
The Washington Papers

... intended to meet the need for authoritative, yet prompt, public appraisal of the major changes in world affairs. Commissioned and written under the auspices of the Center for Strategic and International Studies (CSIS), Georgetown University, Washington, D.C. and published for CSIS by SAGE Publications, Beverly Hills/London.

Series Editor: Walter Laqueur, *Director of the Institute of Contemporary History (London) and Chairman, CSIS, Research Council, Georgetown University*

Price Information: Individual papers in the series are available at $2.50/£1.00 each.

Save on subscriptions: Individuals and institutions can realize substantial savings by entering a subscription order (commencing with Volume I) at the prices given below.

	1 year†	2 year	3 year
Institutional	$20/£8.50	$39/£16.50	$57/£24.00
Individual	$12/£5.40	$23/£10.40	$33/£15.40

†See note on frequency below

Frequency: Volume 1 (September 1972 through December 1973) will include 12 papers published over a 16-month period. Beginning with Volume II (1974). Ten papers will be published each calendar year—and mailed to subscribers in groups of 3 or 4 throughout the year.

Specially commissioned to bring you authoritative evaluations of major events affecting (and affected by) current developments in U.S. foreign policy and world affairs. THE WASHINGTON PAPERS offer timely, provocative, in-depth analyses by leading authorities—who also suggest likely future developments and analyze the policy implications of recent trends.

VOLUME I (1972-73) $2.50 each /£1.00

- WP-1   R. M. Burrell, The Persian Gulf
- WP-2   R. Scalapino, American-Japanese relations in a changing era
- WP-3   E. Luttwak, The strategic balance, 1972
- WP-4   C. Issawi, Oil, the Middle East and the world
- WP-5   W. Laqueur, Neo-isolationism and the world of the seventies
- WP-6   W. E. Griffith, Peking, Moscow and beyond
- WP-7   R. M. Burrell & A. J. Cottrell, Politics, oil and the western Mediterranean
- WP-8   P. Hassner, Europe in the age of negotiation
- WP-9   W. Joshua & W. F. Hahn, Nuclear politics: America, France and Britain

Forthcoming
- WP-10   T. A. Sumberg, Foreign aid as a moral obligation?
- WP-11   H. Block, Trade with the Soviet Union
- WP-12   R. Moss, Hijacking

Sage Professional Papers in **American Politics**

Editor: **Randall B. Ripley,** *Ohio State University.*

VOLUME I (1973)

- 04-001   S. S. Nagel, Comparing elected and appointed judicial systems $2.25/£1.95
- 04-002   J. Dennis, Political socialization research: a bibliography $2.40/£1.00
- 04-003   H. B. Asher, Freshman representatives and the learning of voting cues $2.50/£1.05
- 04-004   J. Fishel, Representation and responsiveness in Congress: "the class of eighty-nine," 1965-1970 $2.70/£1.15

Papers 04-005 through 04-012 to be announced

MAIL TO
SAGE Publications / P.O. Box 5024 / Beverly Hills, Calif. 90210
orders from the U.K., Europe, the Middle East and Africa should be sent to 44 Hatton Garden, London EC1N 8ER